SIMPI
SMALL BATCH BAKING COOKBOOK

The step-by-step guide with sweet and savory recipes for perfect portioned bakes.

MAGERET LAWRENCE

Copyright © [2023] by [MAGERET LAWRENCE]

All rights reserved. No part of this publication may be reproduced, distributed, or transmitted in any form or by any means, including photocopying, recording, or other electronic or mechanical methods, without the prior written permission of the publisher, except in the case of brief quotations embodied in critical reviews and certain other noncommercial uses permitted by copyright law.

This book is a work of nonfiction. While the author has made every effort to provide accurate and up-to-date information, the information contained in this book is provided on an "as is" basis without warranties of any kind, express or implied, including but not limited to the implied warranties of merchantability, fitness for a particular purpose, or non-infringement.

INTRODUCTION 7

Why small batch baking?............................... 9

Tips for successful small batch baking 12

Tools and Equipment 14

Recommended equipment for small batch baking
.... 19

CHAPTER 1 21

Basic Techniques 21

Measuring ingredients accurately 21

Mixing and blending ingredients 23

Baking in small batches 25

CHAPTER 2 27

Cookies recipes 27

Peanut Butter Cookies...................................... 29

Oatmeal Raisin Cookies................................... 32

Sugar Cookies 34

Snickerdoodles... 36

Shortbread Cookies.. 39

Gingerbread Cookies 41

M&M Cookies 43

White Chocolate Macadamia Nut Cookies 45

Ingredients: 45

Almond Butter Cookies 48

CHAPTER 3 51

Bars and Brownies 51

Brownies 51

Lemon bars 53

Raspberry Streusel Bars 56

Blondies 58

S'mores Bars 60

Caramel Apple Bars 62

Chocolate Fudge Bars 64

Cheesecake Bars 66

CHAPTER 4 68

Cakes: 69

Vanilla Cake 69

Chocolate Cake 71

Carrot Cake 73

Red Velvet Cake 76

Lemon Cake 79

Funfetti Cake 81

Pumpkin Cake 83

Strawberry Cake 85

Blueberry Cake 88

Banana Cake 90

CHAPTER 5 92

Breads and Rolls: 93

Banana Bread 93

Pumpkin Bread 95

Zucchini Bread 97

Cinnamon Rolls 99

Dinner Rolls 102

Garlic Knots 104

Bagels 106

Focaccia Bread 108

Irish Soda Bread 110

Pretzels 112

Bonus: 114

How to scale up or down recipes 115

Ideas for using leftover ingredients 117

INTRODUCTION

Mary had always loved baking. From a young age, she would help her mother in the kitchen, mixing ingredients, and watching eagerly as the oven transformed their creations into delicious treats.

As she grew older, her passion for baking only intensified, and she dreamed of one day opening her own bakery.

But Mary knew that starting a full-fledged bakery was no easy feat.

She didn't have the resources or experience to take on such a massive undertaking.

So, she decided to start small.

She began researching small batch baking, a process where you make smaller quantities of baked goods using high-quality ingredients.

Mary was drawn to this approach because it allowed her to experiment with different flavors and techniques without having to invest in expensive equipment or a storefront.

Mary spent hours in the kitchen, tweaking recipes and perfecting her techniques. She experimented with different types of flour, sugars, and flavors until she found the perfect combinations.

Her friends and family were her willing taste testers, providing feedback and encouragement along the way.

As Mary's skills grew, so did her confidence. She started to sell her small batch baked goods at local farmers' markets and pop-up shops. Her customers raved about her products, and soon she had a loyal following.

Word of mouth spread, and Mary's small batch baking business began to take off. She started taking custom orders for weddings, birthdays, and other special events.

People loved the fact that her baked goods were made with high-quality, locally sourced ingredients and that she put so much care and attention into each batch.

Despite the challenges of running a small business, Mary loved every minute of it. She was doing what she loved, and it showed in the quality of her products. Her small batch baking business had become her dream come true, and she knew that with hard work and dedication, it would only continue to grow.

Why small batch baking?

Small batch baking refers to the practice of making smaller quantities of baked goods, typically enough to serve one or two people. While traditional baking recipes often call for larger quantities of ingredients, small batch baking allows for greater flexibility and customization, making it a popular choice for home bakers.

There are several benefits to small batch baking. First, it allows you to experiment with new recipes and ingredients without committing to a large quantity. This can be especially helpful if you're working with expensive or hard-to-find ingredients, or if you're trying out a new technique for the first time.

In addition, small batch baking is a great way to control portion sizes and reduce waste. If you're baking for just one or two people, you don't need to worry about having too many leftovers that may go to waste. This is advantageous for the environment as well as your wallet.

Small batch baking can also be a time-saver, as it typically requires less prep and cooking time than traditional baking. This is especially true if you're using a countertop appliance such as a toaster oven or a mini oven, which can be more energy-efficient and faster than a full-sized oven.

Moreover, small batch baking allows you to personalize your baked goods to your liking.

You can easily adjust the ingredients to suit your preferences or dietary restrictions, and experiment with different flavors and textures.

Finally, small batch baking can be a fun and creative activity to do alone or with friends and family. It's a great way to bond over a shared love of baking, and to indulge in a sweet treat without overindulging.

Overall, small batch baking is a versatile and practical approach to baking that offers numerous benefits. Whether you're an experienced baker or just starting out, small batch baking is a great way to explore your creativity, reduce waste, and enjoy delicious baked goods in smaller quantities.

Tips for successful small batch baking

Small batch baking can be a great way to enjoy fresh-baked goods without the need for excess leftovers. Here are some tips for successful small batch baking:

Use a kitchen scale: small batch baking requires precise measurements, so using a kitchen scale can ensure accurate and consistent results.

Adjust recipe quantities: Reduce recipe quantities to match the size of your small batch. You may need to adjust cooking times and temperatures as well.

Use the right tools: Use smaller baking pans, cookie sheets, or muffin tins to accommodate the smaller batch size.

Preheat the oven: Preheating the oven is essential for small batch baking since the oven will heat up more quickly, which can impact baking times.

Monitor baking times: Keep an eye on the baking time since small batches often require less time in the oven than larger batches.

Keep ingredients at room temperature: For optimal results, bring ingredients like butter, eggs, and milk to room temperature before mixing them together.

Don't rush the cooling process: Let your baked goods cool completely before removing them from the pan. This will ensure that they hold their shape and texture.

Experiment with new recipes: small batch baking provides an opportunity to experiment with new recipes without committing to a large batch. Have fun trying out new recipes and tweaking them to your liking.

Tools and Equipment

Small batch baking can be done with minimal equipment and tools. Here are some essential items to have for small batch baking:

Mixing bowls: Have at least two mixing bowls for mixing ingredients.

Measuring cups and spoons: To accurately measure both dry and liquid ingredients, measuring cups and spoons are necessary.

Hand mixer or Stand mixer: You can use either a hand mixer or stand mixer to mix the ingredients.

Baking sheets or Pans: You will need baking sheets or pans for baking the small batch goods. Choose the size of the pan depending on the recipe you are making.

Silicone mats or Parchment paper: Line the baking sheet or pan with silicone mats or parchment paper to prevent the food from sticking.

Wire racks: Use wire racks to cool the baked goods after they come out of the oven.

Rubber spatulas: Use rubber spatulas to scrape the sides of the mixing bowl and to mix the ingredients evenly.

Whisk: Use a whisk to mix ingredients like eggs, cream, and sauces.

Rolling pin: A rolling pin is essential for rolling out dough for pastries, pie crusts, and cookies.

Pastry brush: Use a pastry brush to brush melted butter, egg wash, and other liquids onto pastries.

These are just some of the basic tools and equipment you will need for small batch baking. Depending on the recipe, you may need additional equipment like a piping bag, food processor, or candy thermometer.

Micro plane or Grater: Use a micro plane or grater to grate lemon or orange zest, chocolate, and other ingredients.

Cookie Cutters: Have a set of cookie cutters in various shapes and sizes for making cookies and pastries.

Muffin or Cupcake Pan: If you plan to make muffins or cupcakes, you will need a muffin or cupcake pan.

Pastry Blender: Use a pastry blender to cut butter or shortening into flour when making pie crusts and other pastries.

Oven thermometer: Use an oven thermometer to check that your oven is set to the proper temperature.

Digital Kitchen Scale: Using a kitchen scale for measuring ingredients can be more accurate than using measuring cups and spoons.

Baking stone: A baking stone can help evenly distribute heat and ensure a crisp crust on bread and pizza.

Cooling rack with feet: Use a cooling rack with feet to allow air to circulate under baked goods, which can help them cool more quickly and prevent sogginess.

Bread knife: A serrated bread knife can be helpful for slicing bread and other baked goods.

Food storage containers: Store your baked goods in airtight food storage containers to keep them fresh.

These tools and equipment can make small batch baking more efficient and enjoyable. However, you don't necessarily need all these items to get started.

Start with the basics and gradually add to your collection as you become more experienced.

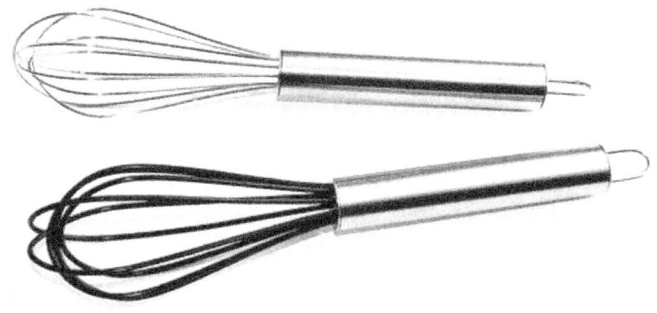

whisk

Recommended equipment for small batch baking

If you're looking to start small-batch baking, you don't need a lot of specialized equipment.

Here are some basic items that can help you get started:

Mixing bowls: You'll need at least one mixing bowl, but it's helpful to have a few in different sizes.

Measuring cups and spoons: Accurate measurements are important in baking, so make sure you have a set of measuring cups and spoons.

Rubber spatula: A rubber spatula is a must-have for scraping the sides of bowls and folding ingredients together.

Whisk: A whisk is great for mixing dry ingredients and for beating eggs and cream.

Baking sheet: A baking sheet is essential for making cookies, and it can also be used for roasting vegetables and toasting nuts.

Rolling pin: If you plan to make pie crusts, cookies, or other baked goods that require rolling, a rolling pin is a must.

Parchment paper: Parchment paper makes clean-up easy and can also be used to line baking sheets and cake pans.

Oven thermometer: An oven thermometer will help you ensure that your oven is at the correct temperature.

Cooling rack: A cooling rack allows air to circulate around baked goods, which helps them cool and prevents them from becoming soggy.

Hand mixer: A hand mixer can be helpful for mixing ingredients together quickly, but it's not essential.

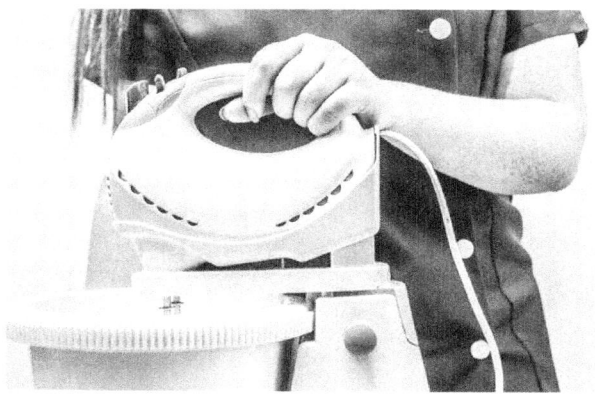

Electric mixer

CHAPTER 1

Basic Techniques

Measuring ingredients accurately

Measuring ingredients accurately is crucial for successful baking, especially when it comes to small batch baking. Here are some tips to help you measure your ingredients accurately:

Use a kitchen scale: A kitchen scale is one of the most accurate ways to measure ingredients. It allows you to weigh ingredients in grams or ounces, which is more precise than measuring by volume.

Use measuring spoons: When measuring small amounts of ingredients like baking powder, baking soda, and salt, use measuring spoons. Make sure to level off the spoon with a straight edge, such as a knife, to ensure accuracy.

Use liquid measuring cups: When measuring liquid ingredients, use a liquid measuring cup. These cups are designed to be filled to the brim and have markings that allow you to accurately measure the amount you need.

Use dry measuring cups: When measuring dry ingredients like flour and sugar, use dry measuring cups. These cups are designed to be filled to the top and leveled off with a straight edge for accuracy.

Don't pack ingredients: When measuring dry ingredients like flour and sugar, avoid packing them into the measuring cup. This can lead to an inaccurate measurement and affect the texture of your baked goods.

Read the recipe carefully: Make sure to read the recipe carefully and follow the instructions for measuring each ingredient. Some recipes may call for ingredients to be measured by weight, while others may require volume measurements.

By following these tips, you can ensure that you are measuring your ingredients accurately, which will result in delicious and perfectly baked treats.

Mixing and blending ingredients

Mixing and blending ingredients properly is an important aspect of small batch baking, as it can affect the texture and flavor of the final product. Here are some techniques you can use to mix and blend ingredients for small batch baking:

Use a whisk: A whisk is great for blending dry ingredients together, such as flour, sugar, and baking powder. Simply whisk the ingredients together in a bowl until they are evenly combined.

Use a fork: If you need to blend butter or shortening into dry ingredients, a fork can work well. Use the tines of the fork to cut the butter into small pieces, and then blend it into the dry ingredients until the mixture resembles coarse crumbs.

Use a spatula: A spatula is great for mixing wet and dry ingredients together. Start by mixing the dry ingredients together in a bowl, then make a well in the center and add the wet ingredients. The wet and dry ingredients should only be barely combined after being gently folded together with a spatula.

Use a stand mixer or hand mixer: If you have a stand mixer or hand mixer, you can use it to mix and blend ingredients quickly and efficiently. Use the paddle attachment to mix dry ingredients together, and the whisk attachment to beat eggs and whip cream.

Use a food processor: A food processor can be used to quickly blend ingredients together, such as making a dough for pie crust. Simply pulse the ingredients together until they are evenly combined.

No matter which technique you use, be sure not to overmix the ingredients, as this can lead to tough, dense baked goods. Mix the ingredients until just combined, then stop and proceed with the recipe.

Baking in small batches

Small batch baking is a great way to satisfy your sweet tooth without overindulging or wasting ingredients. Here are some techniques for successful small batch baking:

Adjust the recipe: Most baking recipes can be easily adjusted to make smaller batches. Divide the ingredients by half or even a quarter, depending on how much you want to make.

Use smaller pans: Use smaller baking pans or ramekins to bake smaller batches. This will help you to avoid wasting ingredients and ensure that your baked goods cook evenly.

Measure accurately: When working with small amounts of ingredients, it's important to measure accurately. Use a kitchen scale to weigh your ingredients or use measuring spoons and cups that are designed for smaller quantities.

Keep an eye on the oven: small batch baking usually requires less time in the oven than larger batches. Keep an eye on your baked goods to ensure that they don't overcook.

Use parchment paper: Line your baking pans or ramekins with parchment paper to prevent sticking and make cleanup easier.

Store leftovers properly: small batches usually mean fewer leftovers, but if you do have extra baked goods, store them in an airtight container to keep them fresh.

By following these techniques, you can enjoy the deliciousness of baking without having to worry about wasting ingredients or overindulging.

CHAPTER 2

Cookies recipes

Chocolate Chip Cookies

Here's a recipe for small-batch chocolate chip cookies that makes about 12 cookies:

Ingredients:

1/4 cup unsalted butter, at room temperature

1/4 cup brown sugar

2 tablespoons granulated sugar

1/2 teaspoon vanilla extract

1 egg yolk

3/4 cup all-purpose flour

1/4 teaspoon baking soda

1/4 teaspoon salt

1/2 cup chocolate chips

Instructions:

Set a baking sheet on the bottom of your oven and preheat it to 350°F (180°C).

In a mixing bowl, cream together the butter, brown sugar, granulated sugar, and vanilla extract until light and fluffy.

Add in the egg yolk and mix until fully incorporated.

The flour, salt, and baking soda should all be combined in a different bowl.

Add the dry ingredients to the mixing bowl with the wet ingredients and mix until just combined.

Fold in the chocolate chips.

Using a cookie scoop or spoon, form the dough into balls and place them onto the prepared baking sheet. Bake for 8 to 10 minutes, until the edges are just beginning to turn golden.

The cookies should cool on the baking sheet for a short while before being moved to a wire rack to finish cooling.

Enjoy your delicious small-batch chocolate chip cookies!

Peanut Butter Cookies

Here's a simple recipe for small batch peanut butter cookies:

Ingredients:

1/4 cup unsalted butter, at room temperature
1/4 cup granulated sugar
1/4 cup brown sugar
1/4 cup creamy peanut butter
1/2 tsp vanilla extract
1 egg yolk
1 cup all-purpose flour
1/2 tsp baking soda
1/4 tsp salt

Instructions:

Preheat your oven to 350°F (175°C). Use parchment paper to cover a baking sheet.

In a mixing bowl, cream together the butter, granulated sugar, and brown sugar until smooth and creamy.

Add the peanut butter, vanilla extract, and egg yolk to the mixture and beat until well combined.

Mix the salt, baking soda, and flour in a different bowl.

Just combine the dry ingredients with the wet mixture after adding them.

Use a cookie scoop or spoon to form balls of dough, about 1 tablespoon each. Place the balls on the prepared baking sheet, leaving 1-2 inches between each cookie.

Use a fork to press down on each ball of dough, creating a crisscross.

pattern on the top of the cookie.

The cookies should be baked for 10 to 12 minutes, or until the edges are just starting to turn golden.

After removing the cookies from the oven, allow them to cool for five minutes on the baking sheet before moving them to a wire rack to finish cooling. This recipe should make around 12-15 small peanut butter cookies. Enjoy!

Oatmeal Raisin Cookies

Here is a recipe for small-batch oatmeal raisin cookies that makes about 6–8 cookies:

Ingredients:

1/2 stick (quarter cup) of unsalted butter, at room temperature

1/4 cup packed light brown sugar

1/4 teaspoon pure vanilla extract

1 large egg yolk

1/2 cup old-fashioned rolled oats

1/4 cup all-purpose flour

1/4 teaspoon baking powder

1/4 teaspoon ground cinnamon

1/8 teaspoon salt

1/4 cup raisins

Instructions:

Preheat the oven to 350°F (180°C). Put parchment paper on a baking sheet.

In a medium bowl, cream the butter and brown sugar together until light and fluffy, about 2 minutes.

Add the vanilla extract and egg yolk and beat until well combined.

In a separate bowl, whisk together the oats, flour, baking powder, cinnamon, and salt.

Mix just until combined after adding the dry ingredients to the wet ones.

Fold in the raisins.

Scoop the dough into 6–8 balls and place them on the prepared baking sheet, spacing them about 2 inches apart.

With the palm of your hand, gently press each ball into the ground.

Bake for 12 to 15 minutes, or until the edges are just starting to turn golden.

The cookies should cool for five minutes on the baking sheet before being moved to a wire rack to finish cooling.

Enjoy your delicious oatmeal raisin cookies!

Sugar Cookies

recipe for small-batch sugar cookies:

Ingredients:

1/2 cup unsalted butter, softened.

1/2 cup granulated sugar

1 egg

1 teaspoon vanilla extract

1 1/2 cups all-purpose flour

1/2 teaspoon baking powder

1/4 teaspoon salt

Instructions:

Preheat the oven to 350°F (180°C) and line a baking sheet with parchment paper.

In a medium bowl, cream the butter and sugar together until light and fluffy.

Beat in the egg and vanilla extract.

Flour, baking soda, and salt should all be combined in separate bowls.

Stirring gradually will ensure a just-combined mixture of the dry and wet ingredients.

Roll the dough into small balls, about 1 tablespoon each, and place them on the prepared baking sheet. Use a fork to gently flatten each ball.

The edges should be lightly golden around 10 to 12 minutes of baking.

The cookies should cool for a few minutes on the baking sheet before being moved to a wire rack to finish cooling.

This recipe makes about 12–14 small cookies. Enjoy!

Snickerdoodles

recipe for small-batch Snickerdoodles:

Ingredients:

1/4 cup unsalted butter, softened.

1/3 cup granulated sugar

1/2 teaspoon vanilla extract

1 large egg yolk

3/4 cup all-purpose flour

1/2 teaspoon cream of tartar

1/4 teaspoon baking soda

1/4 teaspoon salt

For the cinnamon sugar coating:

1 tablespoon granulated sugar

1/2 teaspoon ground cinnamon

Instructions:

Preheat the oven to 350°F (180°C) and line a baking sheet with parchment paper.

In a medium bowl, cream together the softened butter and sugar until light and fluffy, about 2-3 minutes.

Beat in the vanilla extract and egg yolk until well combined.

In a separate small bowl, whisk together the flour, cream of tartar, baking soda, and salt.

Gradually add the dry ingredients to the butter mixture, stirring until just combined.

For the coating, combine the sugar and cinnamon in a small bowl.

Roll the dough into 1-inch balls, then roll each ball in the cinnamon sugar mixture to coat evenly.

The balls should be spaced about 2 inches apart on the baking sheet that has been prepared.

Bake for 10–12 minutes, or until the edges are lightly golden and the cookies are set.

The cookies should cool for five minutes on the baking sheet before being moved to a wire rack to finish cooling.

Enjoy your delicious small-batch Snickerdoodles!

Shortbread Cookies

Here is a recipe for small-batch shortbread cookies:

Ingredients:

1 stick of unsalted butter, half a cup, at room temperature

1/4 cup granulated sugar

1/2 teaspoon vanilla extract

1 cup all-purpose flour

1/8 teaspoon salt

Instructions:

Preheat your oven to 325°F (163°C) and line a baking sheet with parchment paper.

Butter and sugar should be creamed until light and fluffy in a medium bowl.

Once everything is thoroughly combined, add the vanilla extract.

Flour and salt should be combined in a different bowl.

When the dough comes together, add the flour mixture and combine with the butter mixture.

Wrap the dough disk in plastic wrap after forming it. At least 30 minutes should be spent chilling.

Once chilled, roll out the dough on a lightly floured surface to about 1/4-inch thickness.

Cut out the cookies with a cookie cutter and place them on the prepared baking sheet.

Bake for 15-18 minutes, or until the edges of the cookies are lightly golden.

The cookies should cool for a few minutes on the baking sheet before being moved to a wire rack to finish cooling.

Enjoy your delicious small-batch shortbread cookies!

Gingerbread Cookies

Here's a recipe for small-batch gingerbread cookies:

Ingredients:

1/2 cup all-purpose flour

1/4 tsp baking powder

1/4 tsp baking soda

1/4 tsp salt

1/2 tsp ground ginger

1/4 tsp ground cinnamon

2 tbsp unsalted butter, softened

1/4 cup brown sugar, packed

1/4 egg (whisk an egg and use 2 tbsp)

1 tbsp molasses

Instructions:

Preheat the oven to 350°F (180°C). Use parchment paper to cover a baking sheet.

In a small bowl, whisk together flour, baking powder, baking soda, salt, ginger, and cinnamon.

In a separate medium bowl, cream together the softened butter and brown sugar until light and fluffy, about 2 minutes.

Add the egg and molasses to the butter mixture and beat until well combined.

Mix until just combined after adding the dry ingredients in small amounts to the wet mixture.

The dough should be rolled into a disk and then flattened. For at least 30 minutes, place it in the refrigerator, wrapped in plastic wrap.

Once chilled, roll out the dough on a floured surface until it's about 1/4-inch thick. Shapes can be cut out using cookie cutters.

Place the cookies on the prepared baking sheet, leaving about 1 inch between them. Bake for 8 to 10 minutes, or until the edges are just beginning to turn golden.

The cookies should cool for five minutes on the baking sheet before being moved to a wire rack to finish cooling.

Enjoy your small-batch gingerbread cookies!

M&M Cookies

Here's a recipe for M&M cookies that yields about 8-10 cookies:

Ingredients:

1/4 cup unsalted butter, softened.
1/4 cup granulated sugar
1/4 cup brown sugar
1/2 tsp vanilla extract
1 egg yolk
1 cup all-purpose flour
1/2 tsp baking soda
1/4 tsp salt
1/3 cup M&M candies

Instructions:

A baking sheet should be lined with parchment paper, and the oven should be preheated to 350°F (180°C).

Butter that has been softened, sugar, brown sugar, and vanilla extract should all be combined in a mixing bowl and creamed until fluffy.

Once everything is combined, add the egg yolk.

The flour, salt, and baking soda should all be combined in a different bowl.
Gradually add the flour mixture to the butter mixture, mixing until just combined.
Fold in the M&M candies.

Using a cookie scoop or spoon, portion out the cookie dough onto the prepared baking sheet, leaving about 2 inches between each cookie.
The centers should be set and the edges lightly golden after 10 to 12 minutes of baking.

Prior to transferring the cookies to a wire rack to finish cooling, let them cool on the baking sheet for a short while.
Enjoy your homemade M&M cookies!

White Chocolate Macadamia Nut Cookies

Here's a recipe for small-batch White Chocolate Macadamia Nut Cookies:

Ingredients:

1/4 cup unsalted butter, at room temperature

1/4 cup granulated sugar

1/4 cup brown sugar

1/2 teaspoon vanilla extract

1 egg yolk

3/4 cup all-purpose flour

1/4 teaspoon baking soda

1/4 teaspoon salt

1/4 cup white chocolate chips

1/4 cup macadamia nuts, chopped.

Instructions:

Set a baking sheet on the bottom of your oven and preheat it to 350°F (180°C).

Butter, brown sugar, and granulated sugar should be thoroughly combined in a mixing bowl until fluffy.

Beat in the vanilla extract and egg yolk until well combined.

Mix the salt, baking soda, and flour in a different bowl.

Mix until just combined after gradually incorporating the dry ingredients into the wet mixture.

Macadamia nuts and white chocolate chips should be folded in.

Using a cookie scoop or spoon, scoop out the dough and roll it into small balls.

Place the cookie dough balls onto the prepared baking sheet, leaving some space in between each one.

The edges should be lightly golden around 10 to 12 minutes of baking.

The cookies should cool for a few minutes on the baking sheet before being moved to a wire rack to cool completely. Remove the baking sheet from the oven.

Your scrumptious White Chocolate Macadamia Nut Cookies are ready to be served and enjoyed!

This recipe should yield about 10-12 cookies, depending on the size of the cookie dough balls. You can easily double or triple the recipe if you need to make more.

Almond Butter Cookies

Here's a recipe for almond butter cookies that yields about 10-12 cookies:

Ingredients:

1/4 cup almond butter

1/4 cup brown sugar

1/4 cup flour

1/4 tsp baking soda

1/4 tsp salt

1/4 tsp vanilla extract

1 egg

Instructions:

A baking sheet should be lined with parchment paper, and the oven should be preheated to 350°F (175°C).

In a medium bowl, mix the almond butter and brown sugar until well combined.

Until smooth, combine the egg and vanilla extract.

The flour, salt, and baking soda should all be combined in a separate bowl.

Mix just enough to combine the dry ingredients with the wet ones.

The dough should be rolled into 1-inch balls, which you should space about 2 inches apart on the baking sheet you have prepared.

Use a fork to gently press down on the top of each cookie, making a crisscross pattern.

The edges should be golden brown after baking for 10 to 12 minutes.

After the cookies have cooled on the baking sheet for five minutes, move them to a wire rack to finish cooling.

Enjoy your delicious almond butter cookies!

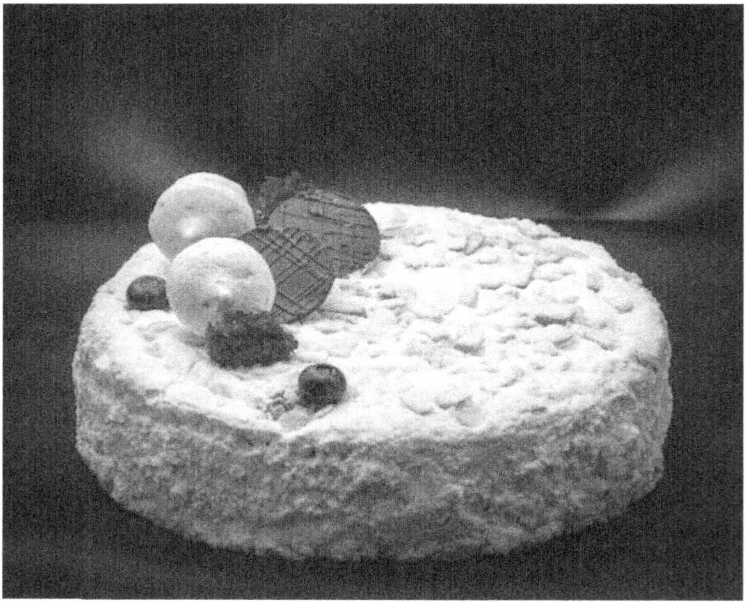

CHAPTER 3

Bars and Brownies

Brownies

Here's a recipe for small-batch brownies that makes about 6-8 servings:

Ingredients:

1/4 cup (4 tablespoons) unsalted butter

1/2 cup granulated sugar

1/4 cup unsweetened cocoa powder

1/4 teaspoon salt

1/2 teaspoon vanilla extract

1 large egg

1/4 cup all-purpose flour

1/4 cup chocolate chips

Instructions:

Preheat your oven to 350°F (175°C). Line an 8-by-8-inch baking pan with parchment paper or foil and set aside.

In a medium-sized microwave-safe bowl, melt the butter in the microwave in 20- to 30-second intervals until fully melted.

To the melted butter, add the sugar, cocoa powder, salt, and vanilla extract. Mix well.

When adding the egg, whisk it in thoroughly.

Add the flour and mix until just combined. Do not overmix.

Fold in the chocolate chips.

The batter should be poured into the prepared pan and the top should be smoothed with a spatula.

When a toothpick is inserted into the center of the brownies, a few moist crumbs should come out with it after 18 to 20 minutes of baking.

Before transferring the brownies to a wire rack to finish cooling, give them 10 minutes to cool in the pan.

Once cool, cut into squares and serve.

Enjoy your delicious homemade brownies!

Lemon bars

Chocolate Paneer's a recipe for small-batch Lemon Bars that makes about 8-10 bars:

Ingredients:

1/2 cup all-purpose flour
2 tablespoons powdered sugar
1/8 teaspoon salt
1/4 cup unsalted butter, chilled and cubed.
1/4 cup granulated sugar
1 large egg yolk
2 tablespoons fresh lemon juice
1/2 teaspoon lemon zest
powdered sugar, for dusting

Instructions:

Preheat your oven to 350°F (175°C). Line an 8x4 inch loaf pan with parchment paper, leaving an overhang on the sides.

Mix the flour, granulated sugar, and salt in a medium bowl. The chilled butter should be incorporated using a pastry cutter or your fingers until the mixture resembles coarse crumbs.

In the loaf pan that has been prepared, press the mixture firmly and evenly. Bake for 10 to 12 minutes, until the edges are just beginning to turn golden.

Meanwhile, in a small bowl, whisk together the granulated sugar, egg yolk, lemon juice, and lemon zest.

Pour the lemon mixture over the baked crust and spread it evenly. Return the pan to the oven and bake for an additional 12-15 minutes, or until the filling is set.

Allow the lemon bars to cool in the pan for 10 minutes, then use the parchment overhang to lift them out of the pan and onto a wire rack to cool completely.

Once the bars are cool, dust with powdered sugar and slice into bars. Enjoy!

Note: You can easily double this recipe to make a larger batch if needed. Ut Butter Bars

Raspberry Streusel Bars

Here's a recipe for Raspberry Streusel Bars that yields a small batch, perfect for small-batch baking:

Ingredients:

1/2 cup all-purpose flour
1/4 cup white sugar
1/8 tsp salt
a quarter cup of small pieces of cold, unsalted butter
1/4 cup rolled oats.
1/4 cup sliced almonds.
1/4 cup raspberry jam

Instructions:

Preheat your oven to 350°F (180°C) and line a 6-inch square baking pan with parchment paper.

Whisk the flour, sugar, and salt in a medium bowl.

The butter should be incorporated using a pastry cutter or your fingers until the mixture resembles coarse crumbs.

Add the rolled oats and sliced almonds and mix until just combined.

Reserve 1/2 cup of the mixture for the streusel topping.

Press the remaining mixture into the bottom of the prepared baking pan, using your hands or the back of a spoon to create an even layer.

Spread the raspberry jam over the crust, leaving a small border around the edges.

Sprinkle the reserved streusel mixture over the jam, pressing it lightly into the jam.

Bake for 25-30 minutes, or until the streusel is golden brown and the jam is bubbly.

Allow the bars to cool completely in the pan, then use the parchment paper to lift them out of the pan.

Cut into squares and serve.

Enjoy your delicious Raspberry Streusel Bars!

Blondies

Blondies are a delicious and easy dessert to make, and they're perfect for small-batch baking. Here's a recipe for blondies that makes just enough for a small group of people.

Ingredients:

1/4 cup unsalted butter, melted.

1/2 cup brown sugar

1 egg

1 tsp vanilla extract

1/2 cup all-purpose flour

1/4 tsp baking powder

1/4 tsp salt

1/4 cup chocolate chips (optional)

Instructions:

Preheat your oven to 350°F (180°C). Grease a 6-inch square baking pan with cooking spray or butter.

In a mixing bowl, combine the melted butter and brown sugar. Mix well.

Add the egg and vanilla extract and mix until well combined.

Add the flour, baking powder, and salt. Avoid overmixing the batter and stir just until combined.

If you're adding chocolate chips, fold them into the batter.

Spread the batter evenly after adding it to the baking pan that has been prepared.

20 to 25 minutes of baking time, or until a toothpick inserted in the center of the cake comes out clean.

Let the blondies cool in the pan for 10 minutes, then remove them from the pan and let them cool completely on a wire rack.

Cut into squares and serve.

Enjoy your delicious homemade blondies!

S'mores Bars

Here's a recipe for small-batch S'mores bars:

Ingredients:

1/2 cup (1 stick) unsalted butter, melted.

1/4 cup granulated sugar

1/4 cup brown sugar

1 egg

1 tsp vanilla extract

1 cup all-purpose flour

1/2 tsp baking powder

1/4 tsp salt

1/2 cup mini chocolate chips

1/2 cup mini marshmallows

2-3 graham crackers, broken into small pieces.

Instructions:

Preheat the oven to 350°F. An 8-by-8-inch baking dish should be greased and set aside.

In a medium-sized mixing bowl, whisk together the melted butter, granulated sugar, and brown sugar until well combined.

Once they are combined, whisk in the egg and vanilla extract.

Salt, baking powder, and flour should all be combined just barely in the bowl.

Fold in the chocolate chips and mini marshmallows.

Evenly spread the batter in the baking dish after pouring it in.

Sprinkle the broken Graham cracker pieces over the top of the batter, pressing them down slightly.

Bake for 20–25 minutes, or until the bars are golden brown and set in the center.

Allow the bars to cool for a few minutes before slicing and serving.

Enjoy your delicious small-batch S'mores bars!

Caramel Apple Bars

Caramel apple bars are a delicious and easy dessert that is perfect for small-batch baking. Here's a recipe you can try:

Ingredients:

1/2 cup all-purpose flour

1/4 cup brown sugar

1/4 teaspoon baking powder

1/8 teaspoon salt

cut into small pieces, two tablespoons of cold, unsalted butter.

1/4 cup chopped pecans.

1/4 cup diced apple.

1/4 cup caramel sauce

Instructions:

Preheat your oven to 350°F (180°C) and line a 8x4 inch (20x10 cm) loaf pan with parchment paper.

The flour, brown sugar, baking soda, and salt should all be mixed in a medium bowl.

Add the cold butter pieces to the bowl and use a pastry cutter or your fingers to work the butter into the dry ingredients until the mixture is crumbly.

Stir in the chopped pecans.

Press the mixture into the bottom of the prepared loaf pan to form an even layer.

Bake for 12–15 minutes, or until the crust is lightly golden brown.

Remove the pan from the oven and sprinkle the diced apple over the crust.

Over the apples, drizzle some caramel sauce.

Return the pan to the oven and bake for an additional 12–15 minutes, or until the caramel is bubbly and the apples are tender.

Allow the bars to cool in the pan for a few minutes before slicing and serving.

Enjoy your delicious and easy Caramel Apple Bars!

Chocolate Fudge Bars

Here's a recipe for chocolate fudge bars that yields a small batch:

Ingredients:

1/4 cup (4 tablespoons) unsalted butter

1/2 cup granulated sugar

1/4 cup unsweetened cocoa powder

1/4 teaspoon salt

1/2 teaspoon vanilla extract

1 large egg

1/2 cup all-purpose flour

Instructions:

Preheat your oven to 350°F (180°C). Put parchment paper on the bottom of an 8-inch square baking pan.

In a medium-sized microwave-safe bowl, melt the butter in the microwave for about 30 seconds. Add in the granulated sugar, cocoa powder, and salt. Stir until well combined.

Add the vanilla extract and egg to the mixture and whisk until the batter becomes smooth and shiny.

Stir in the flour until the batter is smooth and no lumps remain.

Pour the batter into the prepared baking dish, spreading it out evenly.

20 to 25 minutes of baking time, or until a toothpick inserted in the center of the cake comes out clean. Let the chocolate fudge bars cool in the baking dish for 10 minutes before transferring them to a wire rack to cool completely.

After the bars have cooled, cut them into squares and serve.

Enjoy your delicious chocolate fudge bars!

Cheesecake Bars

Cheesecake bars are a delicious and easy dessert that can be made in small batches. Here's a recipe for making 6-8 bars:

Ingredients:

1 cup graham cracker crumbs

2 tbsp sugar

3 tbsp butter, melted.

8 oz cream cheese, softened.

1/3 cup sugar

1 egg

1 tsp vanilla extract

Instructions:

Preheat the oven to 350°F.

The Graham Cracker crumbs, 2 tablespoons of sugar, and melted butter should all be thoroughly combined in a small bowl.

Press the mixture into the bottom of a greased 8-by-8-inch baking dish.

In a medium bowl, beat together the cream cheese and 1/3 cup of sugar until smooth.

Beat after adding the egg and vanilla extract until well combined.

Pour the cheesecake mixture over the graham cracker crust.

When the cheesecake is done, bake for another 25 to 30 minutes.

Refrigerate for at least one hour before serving, then allow to come to room temperature.

Cut into bars and serve.

Enjoy your delicious and creamy cheesecake bars!

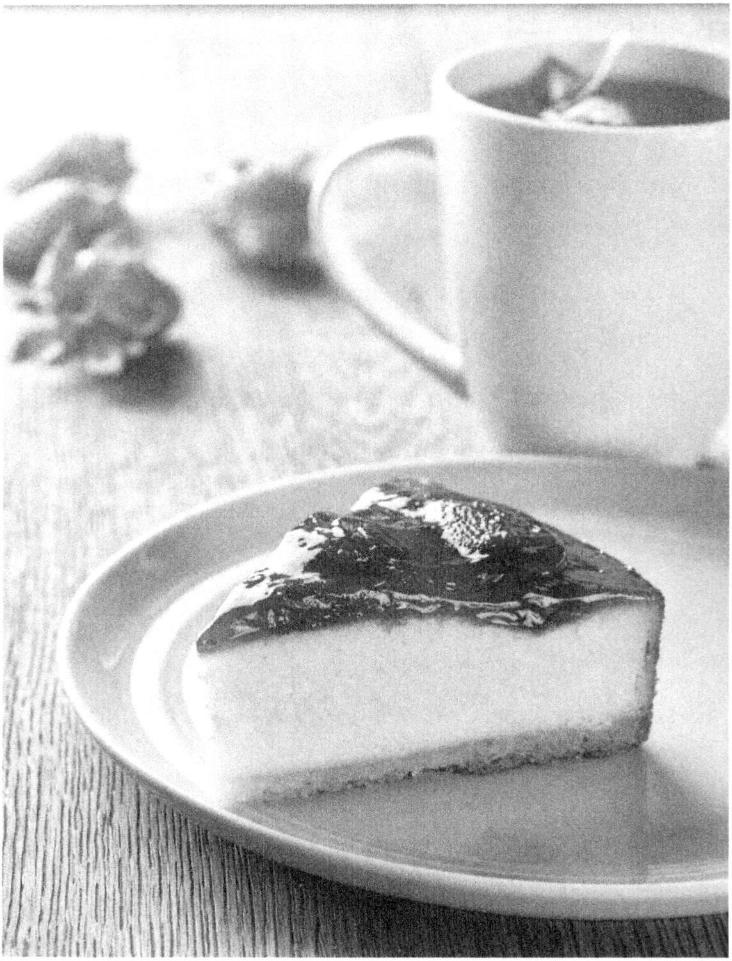

CHAPTER 4

Cakes:

Vanilla Cake

Here's a recipe for a small batch of vanilla cake that yields 6-8 servings:

Ingredients:

1/2 cup all-purpose flour

1/4 cup granulated sugar

1/2 teaspoon baking powder

1/8 teaspoon salt

1/4 cup unsalted butter, softened.

1 egg

1/2 teaspoon vanilla extract

1/4 cup whole milk

Instructions:

Preheat your oven to 350°F (180°C) and grease a 6-inch cake pan with butter or non-stick cooking spray.

In a medium bowl, whisk together the flour, sugar, baking powder, and salt.

Cream the butter and sugar for two to three minutes in a different bowl, until they are light and fluffy.

Add in the egg and vanilla extract and mix until well combined.

Mix until just combined after gradually incorporating the milk in between additions of the flour mixture and the butter mixture.

Pour the batter into the prepared cake pan and bake for 20-25 minutes or until a toothpick inserted into the center of the cake comes out clean.

Allow the cake to cool in the pan for 5 minutes before transferring it to a wire rack to cool completely.

Optional: You can also add frosting or whipped cream on top of the cake for extra sweetness and flavor. Enjoy!

Chocolate Cake

Here is a recipe for a small batch of chocolate cake that serves about 4-6 people:

Ingredients:

1/2 cup all-purpose flour
1/2 cup granulated sugar
1/4 cup unsweetened cocoa powder
1/2 teaspoon baking soda
1/4 teaspoon baking powder
1/4 teaspoon salt
1/4 cup vegetable oil
1/2 teaspoon vanilla extract
1/2 cup warm water
1 egg

Instructions:

Preheat your oven to 350°F (180°C) and grease a 6-inch round cake pan.

The flour, sugar, cocoa powder, salt, baking soda, and all the dry ingredients should be incorporated into a medium bowl.

Add the oil, vanilla extract, and warm water to the dry ingredients and whisk until smooth.

Add the egg and whisk until well combined.

When the cake pan is ready, pour the batter into it. Bake the cake for 25 to 30 minutes, or until a toothpick inserted in the center comes out clean.

The cake should cool in the pan for 5 to 10 minutes before being taken out and placed on a wire rack to finish cooling.

Optional: dust with powdered sugar or frost with your favorite frosting before serving.

Enjoy your delicious and easy-to-make small batch chocolate cake!

Carrot Cake

Here's a recipe for a small batch of carrot cake that serves 4-6 people:

Ingredients:

1/2 cup all-purpose flour
1/2 tsp baking powder
1/4 tsp baking soda
1/4 tsp salt
1/2 tsp ground cinnamon
1/4 tsp ground ginger
1/8 tsp ground nutmeg
1/4 cup vegetable oil
1/4 cup brown sugar
1 large egg
1/2 tsp vanilla extract
1/2 cup finely grated carrots.
1/4 cup chopped walnuts (optional)
Cream cheese frosting:

2 oz cream cheese, softened.

1 tbsp unsalted butter, softened.

1/2 cup powdered sugar

1/4 tsp vanilla extract

Directions:

Preheat the oven to 350°F (180°C). Cake pan with a 6-inch diameter should be greased and lined with parchment paper.

Mix the salt, cinnamon, ginger, nutmeg, baking soda, and flour in a medium bowl.

In a separate bowl, whisk together the vegetable oil, brown sugar, egg, and vanilla extract until smooth.

While whisking, gradually incorporate the dry ingredients into the liquid mixture. Fold in the grated carrots and chopped walnuts, if using.

After pouring the batter into the ready cake pan, use a spatula to level the top.

The cake should be baked for between twenty and twenty-five minutes, or until the center of the cake tester comes out clean.

Before removing the cake from the pan and frosting it, let it cool completely.

Beat the cream, butter, and cheese together until smooth to make the cream cheese frosting. Gradually beat in the powdered sugar and vanilla extract until the frosting is thick and creamy.

After the cake has cooled, cover it with frosting and serve.

Enjoy your delicious small batch carrot cake!

Red Velvet Cake

Here's a recipe for a small batch of red velvet cake that serves 4-6 people:

Ingredients:

1/2 cup all-purpose flour

1/2 cup granulated sugar

1/4 teaspoon baking powder

1/4 teaspoon baking soda

1/4 teaspoon salt

1/4 cup vegetable oil

1/4 cup buttermilk

1 egg

1/2 teaspoon vanilla extract

1/2 teaspoon white vinegar

1 tablespoon cocoa powder

1 tablespoon red food coloring

For the Cream Cheese Frosting:

4 oz cream cheese, softened.

1/4 cup unsalted butter, softened.

1 cup powdered sugar

1/2 teaspoon vanilla extract

Instructions:

Preheat the oven to 350°F (180°C) and line a 6-inch round cake pan with parchment paper.

Mix the flour, sugar, baking soda, baking powder, and salt in a medium mixing bowl.

In another mixing bowl, whisk together the vegetable oil, buttermilk, egg, vanilla extract, white vinegar, cocoa powder, and red food coloring until smooth.

Add the dry ingredients to the wet ingredients and stir until just combined. Do not overmix.

Pour the batter into the prepared cake pan and smooth out the surface.

20 to 25 minutes of baking time, or until a toothpick inserted in the center of the cake comes out clean.

Just before frosting, let the cake cool completely.

For the Cream Cheese Frosting:

In a mixing bowl, beat together the cream cheese and unsalted butter until smooth and creamy.

Add the powdered sugar and vanilla extract and beat until well combined and fluffy.

On top of the cooled cake, evenly distribute the frosting.

Decorate the cake with additional frosting or toppings, if desired.

Enjoy your small batch red velvet cake!

Lemon Cake

Here's a recipe for a small batch of lemon cake that serves about 4-6 people:

Ingredients:

1/2 cup all-purpose flour
1/2 tsp baking powder
1/8 tsp salt
1/4 cup unsalted butter, at room temperature
1/2 cup granulated sugar
1 large egg
1/4 cup whole milk
1 tbsp fresh lemon juice
1 tsp lemon zest

Instructions:

Preheat your oven to 350°F (180°C) and grease a 6-inch cake pan with cooking spray or butter.
Whisk the flour, baking soda, and salt in a medium-sized bowl. Set aside.

Butter and sugar should be creamed until light and fluffy in a separate bowl. Combine well after adding the egg.

Add half of the dry ingredients into the wet ingredients and mix until just combined. Pour in the milk and lemon juice and mix again.

Then, mix until well combined before adding the remaining dry ingredients. Fold in the lemon zest.

Pour the batter into the greased cake pan and bake for 25-30 minutes, or until a toothpick inserted into the center of the cake comes out clean.

The cake should cool in the pan for ten minutes before being moved to a wire rack to finish cooling.

Once the cake is cool, you can dust it with powdered sugar or top it with your favorite frosting or glaze.

Enjoy your delicious lemon cake!

Funfetti Cake

Here's a recipe for a small batch Funfetti cake that yields around 6-8 servings:

Ingredients:

1/2 cup all-purpose flour
1/4 cup granulated sugar
1/2 tsp baking powder
1/4 tsp baking soda
1/4 tsp salt
1/4 cup buttermilk
2 tbsp vegetable oil
1/2 tsp vanilla extract
1/4 cup rainbow sprinkles
1 egg

Instructions:

Preheat the oven to 350°F (180°C).

In a small mixing bowl, whisk together the flour, sugar, baking powder, baking soda, and salt.

In another mixing bowl, whisk together the buttermilk, vegetable oil, vanilla extract, and egg until well combined.

Gradually add the dry ingredients into the wet ingredients, mixing until just combined.

Fold in the rainbow sprinkles.

Put the batter in a 6-inch cake pan that has been greased.

Bake for 20-25 minutes or until a toothpick inserted into the center of the cake comes out clean.

Let the cake cool in the pan for a few minutes before transferring it to a wire rack to cool completely.

Once cooled, you can frost the cake with your favorite frosting and top with more sprinkles if desired. Enjoy!

Pumpkin Cake

Here is a recipe for a small batch pumpkin cake:

Ingredients:

1/2 cup all-purpose flour

1/2 tsp baking powder

1/4 tsp baking soda

1/4 tsp salt

1/2 tsp ground cinnamon

1/4 tsp ground ginger

1/4 tsp ground nutmeg

1/2 cup canned pumpkin puree.

1/4 cup granulated sugar

1/4 cup vegetable oil

1 egg

Instructions:

Preheat your oven to 350°F (180°C). Grease and flour a 6-inch round cake pan.

Flour, baking powder, baking soda, salt, cinnamon, ginger, and nutmeg should all be combined in a standard size mixing bowl.

In a separate mixing bowl, whisk together the pumpkin puree, sugar, oil, and egg.

Then, just combine the mixture by whisking in the dry ingredients after adding the wet ones.

Using the prepared cake pan, pour the batter into it.

When a toothpick is inserted into the center of the cake, it should come out clean after 25 to 30 minutes of baking.

Allow the cake to cool in the pan for 5 minutes, then transfer it to a wire rack to cool completely.

You can top the cake with whipped cream, cream cheese frosting, or a dusting of powdered sugar if desired. Enjoy!

Strawberry Cake

Here's a recipe for a small batch of strawberry cake that serves around 4-6 people:

Ingredients:

1/2 cup all-purpose flour
1/4 cup granulated sugar
1/2 teaspoon baking powder
1/8 teaspoon baking soda
1/8 teaspoon salt
1/4 cup milk
2 tablespoons unsalted butter, melted.
1/2 teaspoon vanilla extract
1/4 cup chopped fresh strawberries.
1 egg
For the frosting:

1/4 cup unsalted butter, at room temperature
1 cup powdered sugar
1/4 teaspoon vanilla extract
1 tablespoon milk

Fresh strawberries for garnish

Instructions:

Preheat the oven to 350°F (180°C) and grease a 6-inch cake pan.

In a medium bowl, whisk together the flour, sugar, baking powder, baking soda, and salt.

In another bowl, whisk together the milk, melted butter, vanilla extract, and egg.

Just combine the dry ingredients with the wet ingredients after adding them.

Fold in the chopped strawberries.

When the cake pan is ready, pour the batter into it.

Bake the cake for twenty to twenty-five minutes, until a toothpick inserted inside the center comes out clean.

Let the cake cool in the pan for 5 minutes before transferring it to a wire rack to cool completely.

For the frosting:

In a medium bowl, cream the butter with an electric mixer until smooth.

Add the powdered sugar, vanilla extract, and milk, and mix until smooth and creamy.

Once the cake is completely cool, spread the frosting over the top of the cake and garnish with fresh strawberries.

Enjoy your delicious small batch strawberry cake!

Blueberry Cake

Here's a recipe for blueberry cake for small batch baking that makes enough for 4-6 servings:

Ingredients:

1/2 cup all-purpose flour

1/4 cup granulated sugar

1/2 tsp baking powder

1/4 tsp salt

1/4 cup milk

2 tbsp unsalted butter, melted.

1/2 tsp vanilla extract

1/2 cup fresh blueberries

Instructions:

Preheat your oven to 350°F (175°C). Grease a 6-inch round cake pan or a small loaf pan with butter or cooking spray.

The flour, sugar, baking soda, and salt should be combined in a medium bowl.

In a separate small bowl, mix the milk, melted butter, and vanilla extract.

Mix the dry ingredients just enough to combine after adding the wet ingredients.

Gently fold in the blueberries.

Using a spatula, level the top after pouring the batter into the prepared pan.

A piece of wood inserted into the middle of the cake should finally came out clean after 20 to 25 minutes of baking.

Allow the cake to cool for a few minutes in the pan, then transfer it to a wire rack to cool completely.

Slice and serve the cake once it has cooled.

Enjoy your delicious and easy blueberry cake for small batch baking!

Banana Cake

Here's a recipe for a small batch of banana cake:

Ingredients:

1 ripe banana
1/4 cup all-purpose flour
1/4 cup granulated sugar
1/4 teaspoon baking powder
1/4 teaspoon baking soda
1/8 teaspoon salt
1/4 teaspoon vanilla extract
1 egg
2 tablespoons vegetable oil

Instructions:

Preheat your oven to 350°F (175°C) and line a small loaf pan with parchment paper.

In a mixing bowl, mash the banana with a fork until it's smooth.

Add the flour, sugar, baking powder, baking soda, salt, vanilla extract, egg, and vegetable oil. Up until a simple combination, combine everything.

Fill the loaf pan with the batter and use a spatula to smooth the top.

A toothpick inserted in the center of the cake should come out clean after 20 to 25 minutes of baking it in the preheated oven.

After the cake has finished cooling in the pan, move it to a wire rack to finish cooling.

Serve the banana cake as is or with your favorite frosting or glaze.

Enjoy your delicious and easy-to-make small batch banana cake!

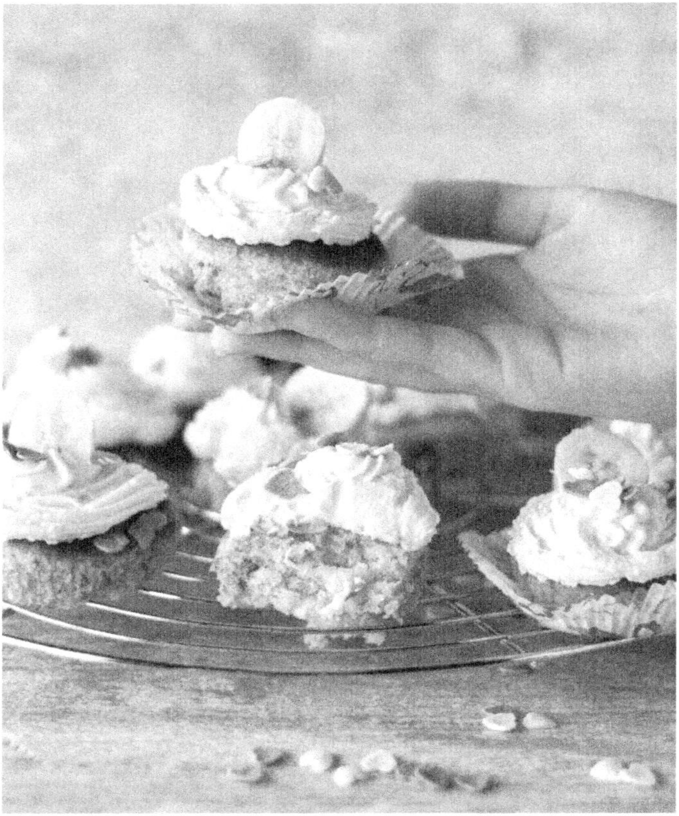

CHAPTER 5

Breads and Rolls:

Banana Bread

Ingredients:

1 ripe banana, mashed.

1/4 cup sugar

1/4 cup vegetable oil

1/2 tsp vanilla extract

1 egg

1/2 cup all-purpose flour

1/4 tsp baking soda

1/4 tsp baking powder

1/4 tsp salt

Instructions:

Preheat your oven to 350°F (180°C).

Grease a small loaf pan with butter or cooking spray.

In a medium-sized mixing bowl, mash the ripe banana until it's smooth.

Add the sugar, vegetable oil, vanilla extract, and egg. Mix until well combined.

Combine the flour, baking soda, baking powder, and salt in a different mixing bowl.

Combine just until combined after gradually incorporating the dry ingredients into the wet ones.

Put the ready loaf pan with the batter inside.

A toothpick embedded into the center of the bread should come out clean after twenty-five to thirty minutes of baking.

Let the bread cool in the pan for a few minutes before removing it from the pan and transferring it to a wire rack to cool completely.

Enjoy your delicious small batch banana bread!

Pumpkin Bread

Here's a recipe for pumpkin bread that makes a small batch, perfect for baking in a loaf pan.

Ingredients:

1/2 cup pumpkin puree

1/4 cup vegetable oil

1/2 cup sugar

1 egg

1/2 teaspoon vanilla extract

3/4 cup all-purpose flour

1/2 teaspoon baking soda

1/4 teaspoon baking powder

1/4 teaspoon salt

1/2 teaspoon ground cinnamon

1/4 teaspoon ground ginger

1/4 teaspoon ground nutmeg

Instructions:

Preheat the oven to 350°F (175°C). A spread loaf pan should be greased with butter or cooking spray.

Pumpkin puree, vegetable oil, sugar, egg, and vanilla extract should all be thoroughly merged in a medium bowl.

Mix the flour, baking soda, baking powder, salt, cinnamon, ginger, and nutmeg in a separate bowl.

Stir just till combined after adding the flour mixture to the wet ones.

Fill the loaf pan with the batter and use a spatula to smooth the top.

A piece of wood inserted into the center of the bread should come out clean after 35 to 40 minutes of baking.

After letting the bread cool in the pan for ten minutes, take it out and place it on a wire rack to finish cooling.

Enjoy your delicious homemade pumpkin bread!

Zucchini Bread

Zucchini bread is a delicious and easy-to-make treat that's perfect for small batch baking. Here's a recipe for making zucchini bread in small quantities:

Ingredients:

1 small zucchini, grated (about 1 cup)
1/4 cup vegetable oil
1/2 cup granulated sugar
1/2 teaspoon vanilla extract
1 egg
1 cup all-purpose flour
1/2 teaspoon baking powder
1/4 teaspoon baking soda
1/2 teaspoon ground cinnamon
1/4 teaspoon salt

Instructions:

Preheat your oven to 350°F (175°C). Grease and flour a 6x3 inch loaf pan.

In a medium mixing bowl, combine the grated zucchini, vegetable oil, sugar, vanilla extract, and egg. Mix until well combined.

In a separate mixing bowl, whisk together the flour, baking powder, baking soda, cinnamon, and salt.

Mix just enough to combine the dry ingredients with the wet ones. Do not overmix.

After smoothing the top, pour the batter into the loaf pan that has been prepared.

A toothpick inserted in the center should come out clean after baking for 35 to 40 minutes.

After the bread has cooled in the pan for ten minutes, remove it from the pan and set it on a wire rack to finish cooling.

Enjoy your delicious zucchini bread in small batches!

Cinnamon Rolls

here's a recipe for small batch cinnamon rolls:

Ingredients:

1 cup all-purpose flour
1 tbsp granulated sugar
1/2 tsp active dry yeast
1/4 cup milk
1 tbsp unsalted butter
1/4 tsp salt
1/4 tsp vanilla extract
For the filling:

1 tbsp unsalted butter, softened.
2 tbsp brown sugar
1 tsp cinnamon
For the glaze:

1/2 cup powdered sugar

1 tbsp milk

1/4 tsp vanilla extract

Instructions:

Combine the flour, sugar, yeast, and salt in a mixing bowl.

Milk and butter should be heated in a small saucepan over low heat until the butter has melted. Add vanilla after removing from the heat.

Pour the milk mixture into the flour mixture and stir until well combined and a dough forms.

The dough should be smoothed out by 5 minutes of kneading on a floured surface.

Roll out the dough into a rectangle about 1/4 inch thick.

Butter should be softened and applied to the dough's surface.

Combine cinnamon and brown sugar in a small bowl. Sprinkle this mixture over the buttered surface of the dough.

Roll up the dough tightly, starting from the short end.

Cut the rolled-up dough into 4-6 pieces.

Place the cinnamon rolls in a greased baking dish, leaving a little space between each roll.

The dish should rise in a warm spot for about 30 minutes after being covered with a kitchen towel.

Preheat your oven to 350°F (180°C).

Bake the cinnamon rolls for 15-20 minutes, or until golden brown.

While the cinnamon rolls are baking, whisk together powdered sugar, milk, and vanilla extract to make the glaze.

Once the cinnamon rolls are done baking, remove them from the oven and let them cool for a few minutes. Drizzle the glaze over the top of the cinnamon rolls and serve warm.

Enjoy your homemade small-batch cinnamon rolls!

Dinner Rolls

Here's a recipe for dinner rolls that makes a small batch, perfect for small-scale baking:

Ingredients:

1/2 cup warm water
1 tsp active dry yeast
1 tbsp sugar
1/2 tsp salt
1 1/2 cups all-purpose flour
2 tbsp unsalted butter, melted.
1 egg, beaten.

Instructions:

Warm water, sugar, and yeast should all be combined in a small bowl. Stir to dissolve the yeast and let sit for 5 minutes, or until foamy.

In a medium bowl, whisk together the flour and salt. Add the melted butter, beaten egg, and yeast mixture to the flour mixture. Stir until the dough comes together.

The dough should be smooth and elastic after 5 minutes of kneading it on a floured surface.

The dough should be put in a lubricated bowl, covered with a wet cloth, and allowed to rise for an hour, or until it has doubled in size, in a warm location.

Bake at 375°F (190°C) for 15 minutes on a parchment-lined baking sheet.

Punch down the dough and divide it into 8 equal pieces. Each piece should be formed into a ball, then placed on the baking sheet.

Cover the rolls with a damp cloth and let them rise in a warm place for 30 minutes, or until puffy.

Bake for 15-20 minutes, or until golden bro.

Garlic Knots

here's a recipe for garlic knots that yields about 12 small knots:

Ingredients:

1 cup all-purpose flour
1 tsp instant yeast
1/2 tsp salt
1/2 tsp sugar
1/3 cup warm water
2 tbsp olive oil
1 clove garlic, minced.
1 tbsp butter, melted.
1 tbsp chopped fresh parsley (optional)

Instructions:

Flour, yeast, salt, and sugar should all be combined in a mixing bowl.

Add the warm water and olive oil to the bowl. Mix until the dough comes together.

For approximately 5 minutes, knead the dough until it is elastic and smooth on a lightly dusted flour surface.

Place the dough in a lightly oiled bowl, cover with a towel, and let it rise in a warm place for about 1 hour, until it doubles in size.

Preheat the oven to 375°F (190°C).

Divide the dough into 12 equal portions and roll each one into a rope about 6 inches long.

Tie each rope into a knot and place them on a baking sheet lined with parchment paper.

Melted butter and garlic powder should be combined in a small bowl. Brush the garlic butter over the knots.

Bake the knots for 12-15 minutes, until they're golden brown.

Optional: Sprinkle chopped fresh parsley over the knots before serving.

Enjoy your delicious homemade garlic knots!

Bagels

Here is a recipe for small batch bagels that yields about 4-6 bagels:

Ingredients:

1 cup bread flour

1 tsp instant yeast

1/2 tsp salt

1/2 tbsp sugar

1/4 cup warm water

1 tbsp vegetable oil

1 egg, beaten.

Any desired toppings (sesame seeds, poppy seeds, etc.)

Instructions:

In a large mixing bowl, combine the bread flour, yeast, salt, and sugar. Mix well.

Add the warm water and vegetable oil to the bowl and mix until a dough forms.

The dough should be smooth and elastic after 5 to 10 minutes of kneading.

The dough should be placed in a lightly oiled bowl, covered with plastic wrap or a damp towel, and allowed to rise for an hour or until doubled in size in a warm location.

For best results, line a baking sheet with parchment paper and preheat the oven to 425°F (220°C).

Create balls out of each of the 4-6 equal pieces of dough.

With your finger, make a hole in the center of each ball, then gently stretch the dough to form a bagel shape.

Place the bagels on the lined baking sheet and let them rest for 10-15 minutes.

Brush the beaten egg over the top of each bagel and sprinkle with your desired toppings.

Bake the bagels for 15-20 minutes, or until golden brown and cooked through.

Remove from the oven and allow to cool before serving.

Enjoy your homemade bagels!

Focaccia Bread

Here's a recipe for making a small batch of focaccia bread:

Ingredients:

1 1/4 cups all-purpose flour

1/2 tsp salt

1/2 tsp active dry yeast

2/3 cup warm water

1 tbsp olive oil

Toppings of your choice (such as herbs, garlic, cherry tomatoes, olives, or cheese)

Instructions:

Flour, salt, and yeast should be combined in a sizable mixing bowl.

Add the warm water and olive oil to the bowl and stir until a shaggy dough forms.

The dough should be smooth and elastic after being turned out onto a floured surface and kneaded for 5 to 10 minutes.

Place the dough back in the mixing bowl, cover with a clean towel, and let rise for 1-2 hours, until the dough has doubled in size.

Preheat your oven to 425°F (218°C) and line a baking sheet with parchment paper.

Once the dough has risen, gently punch it down and shape it into a flat disk or rectangle that fits your baking sheet.

Transfer the dough to the prepared baking sheet and use your fingertips to make dimples all over the surface of the dough.

Drizzle the top of the dough with olive oil and sprinkle with your desired toppings.

Bake for 20-25 minutes, until the bread is golden brown and cooked through.

Serve warm or at room temperature.

Enjoy your freshly baked focaccia bread!

Irish Soda Bread

Irish soda bread is a delicious and easy-to-make bread that requires no yeast and can be baked in a small batch. Here's a recipe for a small batch of Irish soda bread that makes one loaf.

Ingredients:

1 1/2 cups all-purpose flour

1/2 cup whole wheat flour

1 teaspoon baking soda

1/2 teaspoon salt

1/2 tablespoon sugar

1 tablespoon butter, softened.

1/2 cup buttermilk

Instructions:

Preheat your oven to 375°F (190°C) and line a small baking sheet with parchment paper.

In a mixing bowl, whisk together the all-purpose flour, whole wheat flour, baking soda, salt, and sugar until well combined.

Cut the butter into small pieces and use a pastry cutter or your fingers to work the butter into the flour mixture until the mixture resembles coarse crumbs.

To add the buttermilk, create a well in the middle of the flour mixture.

Stir until the mixture is just combined and forms a dough. The dough will be slightly sticky.

Turn the dough out onto a floured surface and knead it gently for 1-2 minutes until it comes together into a round loaf.

Place the loaf onto the prepared baking sheet and use a sharp knife to make a cross-shaped cut on the top of the loaf. This helps the bread to cook evenly.

The bread should be baked for 30-35 minutes, or until golden brown and hollow when tapped on the bottom.

Allow the bread to cool on a wire rack for at least 10 minutes before slicing and serving.

Enjoy your delicious homemade Irish soda bread!

Pretzels

Here's a recipe for homemade pretzels that yields a small batch:

Ingredients:

1 cup all-purpose flour

1/2 teaspoon salt

1/2 teaspoon instant yeast

1/4 cup warm water

1 tablespoon vegetable oil

1 tablespoon baking soda

1/2 cup hot water

Coarse salt for sprinkling

Instructions:

In a mixing bowl, combine flour, salt, and yeast.

Add warm water and vegetable oil to the bowl and stir to form a dough.

The dough needs to be smooth and elastic after 5 minutes of kneading on a lightly dusted surface.

Place the dough in a greased bowl, cover it with a damp cloth, and let it rise in a warm place for 30 minutes.

Preheat the oven to 425°F (220°C).

Mix hot water and baking soda in a small bowl.

The dough should be divided into 4 equal pieces.

Roll each piece into a long rope.

Shape each rope into a pretzel by forming a loop, twisting the ends around each other, and then folding the twisted ends down to the bottom of the loop.

Dip each pretzel into the baking soda solution and place it on a baking sheet lined with parchment paper.

Sprinkle coarse salt over the pretzels.

Bake the pretzels in the preheated oven for 10-12 minutes, or until golden brown.

Serve warm.

Enjoy your homemade pretzels!

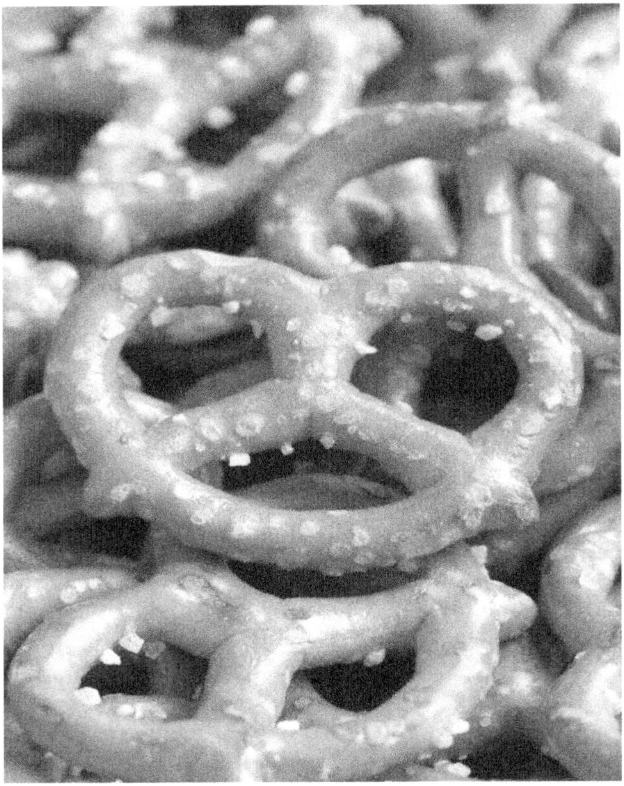

Bonus:

How to scale up or down recipes

Scaling recipes up or down is a common practice in cooking and baking, and it can be done easily with a little bit of math. Here are some general tips for scaling recipes for a small batch baking cookbook:

Determine the conversion factor: To scale a recipe up or down, you need to determine the conversion factor. This is the ratio of the original recipe to the new recipe. For example, if you want to make a recipe half its original size, the conversion factor would be 0.5.

Adjust the ingredients: Multiply or divide each ingredient in the recipe by the conversion factor. For example, if the original recipe calls for 2 cups of flour and you want to make a half batch, you will use 1 cup of flour instead. If you are scaling up, you would multiply the ingredient amounts by the conversion factor.

Adjust the baking time: baking times may need to be adjusted when scaling recipes.

Check the recipe regularly and adjust the baking time as needed.

Adjust the pan size: If you are scaling a recipe up or down, you may need to adjust the size of the baking pan to accommodate the new recipe.

A larger or smaller pan may affect the baking time and the texture of the final product.

Test and adjust: Whenever you scale a recipe, it's a good idea to test it first before serving it to others. This will give you an idea of any adjustments that need to be made to the recipe for the best results.

Remember to keep track of the changes you make to the recipe so you can reproduce it consistently in the future.

Ideas for using leftover ingredients.

If you're someone who enjoys baking, then you're likely to have a few leftover ingredients lying around in your kitchen from time to time.

Instead of letting those ingredients go to waste, why not get creative and use them in small-batch baking?

Here are some ideas for using leftover ingredients for a small-batch baking cookbook:

Chocolate Chips: Chocolate chips are a staple ingredient in baking, and you might find yourself with leftover chips after making a batch of cookies. Use them up by making a small batch of chocolate chip muffins or scones. You can also mix them into pancake or waffle batter for a delicious breakfast treat.

Overripe Bananas: Bananas that are past their prime are perfect for making banana bread. But if you don't have enough bananas for a full loaf, you can still make a small batch of banana muffins or pancakes. You can also use mashed bananas as a sweetener in oatmeal or smoothie bowls.

Nuts: If you have leftover nuts, like almonds or walnuts, you can use them in a variety of baked goods.

Try making a small batch of nutty granola bars or adding them to muffin or bread batter. You can also make a small batch of nut butter or sprinkle chopped nuts over ice cream or yogurt.

Citrus Zest: If you have leftover citrus zest, like lemon or orange, you can use it to add flavor to baked goods. Try making a small batch of citrus shortbread cookies or adding zest to scones or muffins. You can also use citrus zest to flavor homemade whipped cream or frosting.

Buttermilk: If you have leftover buttermilk, you can use it in a variety of baked goods. Try making a small batch of buttermilk biscuits or pancakes. You can also use buttermilk to make a small batch of ranch dressing or as a marinade for chicken.

Leftover Cereal: If you have leftover cereal, you can use it to make a small batch of cereal bars or granola. You can also crush the cereal and use it as a coating for chicken or fish.

Mix it into cookie or muffin batter for a unique twist on traditional recipes.

Jam or Jelly: If you have leftover jam or jelly, you can use it to make thumbprint cookies or add it to muffin or cake batter for a fruity twist. You can also use jam as a glaze for roasted meats or as a topping for pancakes or waffles.

Sour Cream: If you have leftover sour cream, you can use it to make a small batch of sour cream coffee cake or muffins. You can also use it to make a creamy pasta sauce or as a dip for vegetables or chips.

Leftover Bread: If you have leftover bread, you can use it to make a small batch of bread pudding or croutons for salads. You can also make a small batch of French toast or use it to make homemade breadcrumbs for meatballs or meatloaf.

Leftover Vegetables: If you have leftover vegetables, like carrots or zucchini, you can use them to make a small batch of vegetable muffins or bread. You can also chop them up and use them as a topping for pizza or mix them into pasta dishes for added nutrition.

In conclusion, using leftover ingredients for small-batch baking is not only a creative way to reduce food waste, but it also provides an opportunity to experiment with new flavors and textures.

With these ideas, you can turn your leftovers into delicious baked goods that your family and friends will love.

Recipe:

Ingredients:

Notes

Recipe: ....

Ingredients: ....

....
....
....
....
....
....
....
....
....
....
....
....
....
....
....
....

Notes

....
....
....

Recipe: ....

Ingredients: ....

....
....
....
....
....
....
....
....
....
....
....
....
....
....
....
....
....

Notes

....
....
....

Recipe: ....

Ingredients: ....

....
....
....
....
....
....
....
....
....
....
....
....
....
....
....
....

Notes

....
....
....

Recipe: ....

Ingredients: ....

....
....
....
....
....
....
....
....
....
....
....
....
....
....
....
....

Notes

....
....
....

Recipe:

Ingredients:

Notes

Recipe:..

Ingredients:..

....
....
....
....
....
....
....
....
....
....
....
....
....
....
....

Notes

....
....
....

Recipe: ....

Ingredients: ....

....
....
....
....
....
....
....
....
....
....
....
....
....
....
....

Notes

....
....
....

Recipe:..

Ingredients:..

....

....

....

....

....

....

....

....

....

....

....

....

....

....

....

Notes

Recipe:

Ingredients:

Notes

Recipe:

Ingredients:

Notes

Recipe: ....

Ingredients: ....

Notes

Recipe: ....

Ingredients: ....

....
....
....
....
....
....
....
....
....
....
....
....
....
....
....

Notes

....
....
....

Recipe: ....

Ingredients: ....

....
....
....
....
....
....
....
....
....
....
....
....
....
....
....
....

Notes

....
....
....

Recipe: ....

Ingredients: ....

Notes

Recipe: ....

Ingredients: ....

....

....

....

....

....

....

....

....

....

....

....

....

....

....

....

....

Notes

....

....

....

Recipe:

Ingredients:

Notes

Recipe:

Ingredients:

Notes

Recipe:

Ingredients:

Notes

Recipe:

Ingredients:

Notes

Printed in Great Britain
by Amazon